Jokes for Kids

The big book of silly jokes for kids

Table of Contents

Introduction 1

Chapter 1: Jokes for Kids 2

Conclusion 49

Introduction

Thank you for taking the time to read this book full of silly jokes!

This book contains hundreds of the funniest and silliest jokes that will have the whole family laughing!

Enjoy sharing these jokes with your friends and family, and see how much you can make them laugh!

Once again, thanks for picking up this book, I hope you enjoy it!

Chapter 1: Jokes for Kids

Where does a General keep his armies?

In his sleevies!

What did the grape say when it was crushed?

Nothing, it just let out a little wine.

Why did the birdie go to the hospital?

For a little tweetment.

How does an octopus go into battle?

Well-armed.

What's the best thing about Switzerland?

I'm not sure, but their flag is a big plus!

Where do you find a cow with no legs?

Right where you left it.

Why aren't koalas considered to be actual bears?

They don't have the koalafications.

What's ET short for?

Because he has little legs.

Why was the octopus laughing?

Because of ten tickles (tentacles)

Why did the turkey refuse to eat on Thanksgiving Day?

Because it was stuffed.

How does a musician clean his dirty tuba?

He uses a tuba toothpaste!

Why did Goldilocks wake up scared in the middle of the night?

Because she had night bears.

Where does a butterfly like to sleep?

On a cater-pillow

What is a bumblebee's favorite type of music?

Bee-Bop

Why do birds fly to warmer climates in Winter?

It's much easier than walking!

How does the ocean say hello?

It waves.

What did one plate whisper to the other?

Dinner is on me!

Why can't dogs dance?

They have 2 left feet!

What do you call an old snowman?

Water.

What do Alexander the Great and Winnie the Pooh have in common?

They have the same middle name.

What do you call a bear with no ears?

B-

Why did the banana go to the hospital?

He was peeling really bad!

Why was the photo sent to prison?

He was framed!

Which superhero is the best at hitting home runs?

Batman.

What do you call a boomerang that doesn't come back?

A stick.

Why did the tomato blush?

Because it saw the salad dressing.

Why was the math book sad?

Because of all its problems.

How do you make holy water?

You boil the hell out of it!

Why did the bicycle fall over?

It was two-tired

Why was the sand wet?

Because the sea weed.

What do you call a magical dog?

A labracadabrador.

What's orange and sounds like a parrot?

A carrot.

How do you make an artichoke?

You strangle it!

What key is the best for opening a banana?

A monkey.

What did one wall say to the other wall?

I'll meet you at the corner!

What do you call a bear with no teeth?

A gummy bear.

Where do cows go for fun?

To the moo-vies.

What do you call a cow with no legs?

Ground beef.

What do you call a pig that knows karate?

Pork chop.

Why do bees have sticky hair?

Because they use honey-combs.

What animal needs to wear a wig?

A bald eagle.

What do you call a fly without wings?

A walk.

Where do fish keep their money?

In the river bank!

What's brown and sticky?

A stick.

What side of a chicken has the most feathers?

The outside!

Why did the cookie go to the hospital?

Because he felt crummy.

What did one hat say to the other?

You stay here, I'm going on ahead.

What shoes do ninjas wear?

Sneakers!

Why did the girl throw a clock out the window?

Because she wanted to see time fly!

Which hand is the best to write with?

Neither. It's better to write with a pen.

What is a wizard's favorite subject at school?

Spelling.

What kind of haircuts do bees get?

Buzzzzzzzz cuts

What do you call a sleeping dinosaur?

Dino-snore.

What did the right eye say to the left eye?

Between us, something smells!

What do you get when you cross a vampire and a snowman?

Frost-bite!

Why did the student eat her homework?

Because her teacher said it was a piece of cake!

Why is 6 afraid of 7?

Because 7-8-9 (seven ate nine).

What kind of tree can you fit in your hand?

A palm tree.

What falls every Winter but never gets hurt?

Snow.

What did the volcano say to his girlfriend?

I lava you!

What's a tornado's favorite game?

Twister!

What's worse than finding a worm in your apple?

Finding half a worm.

What did the nose say to the finger?

Stop picking on me!

Why didn't the skeleton go to prom?

He had no body to dance with.

What do you call a fake noodle?

An im-pasta!

Why do mountains make good comedians?

They're hill-arious

Why are ghosts terrible at lying?

You can see right through them.

Why did the orange lose the race?

Because he ran out of juice.

What's a pirate's favorite letter?

Arrrrrrrr

What did the number 0 say to the number 8?

Nice belt!

What do you call a fish with no eyes?

A fsh.

Where do elephants keep their clothes?

In their trunks.

Why was the broom late to work?

It over-swept.

What is a ghost's favorite food?

I scream!

Where do sheep go for vacation?

The baa-hamas.

Why do birds fly?

It's much faster than walking!

What time do ducks wake up?

At the quack of dawn.

What did the traffic light say to the car?

Don't look, I'm changing!

What do you call an owl who does magic tricks?

Who-dini.

Why do you never see elephants hiding in trees?

Because they're really good at it!

How do you pay for parking in space?

A parking meteor.

Why animal can jump higher than the Statue of Liberty?

All of them. The Statue of Liberty can't jump!

Have you heard the rumor going around about butter?

Never mind, I shouldn't spread it.

What do you call cheese that isn't yours?

Nacho cheese.

What did the potato say to the mushroom?

You're a fun guy (fungi).

What do you call an alligator that has a magnifying glass?

An investigator.

What do you get when you pamper a cow?

Spoiled milk.

What do you call a sleeping bull?

A bull-dozer.

What do you call a sheep with no legs?
A cloud.

What kind of bow can't be tied?
A rainbow.

What did one snowman say to the other?
Can you smell carrots?

Why did the toilet paper roll down the hill?
To get to the bottom.

Why was Eeyore in the bathroom?

Because he was looking for Pooh!

Why do sharks live in salt?

Because pepper water makes them sneeze!

What clothes does a cloud wear?

Thunderwear.

What did the fish monger say to the magician?

Pick a cod, any cod...

Why does Cinderella never win soccer?

Because she's always running away from the ball!

How does Darth Vader like his toast cooked?

On the dark side.

What kind of room doesn't have any doors?

A mushroom.

Why did the golfer wear two pairs of pants?

In case he got a hole-in-one.

What's a cow's favorite holiday?

Moo year's eve.

Did you hear the joke about the roof?

Never mind, it'll go over your head!

What did the envelope say to stamp?

Stick with me and together we'll go places.

What has legs but can't walk?

A pair of pants.

What do you call a bear who has no teeth?

A gummy bear.

Why are fish so smart?

Because they're always in schools.

How do snails fight?

They slug it out!

Why are cats so bad at telling stories?

They only have one tail!

How do cats bake muffins?

From scratch.

Why doesn't the shrimp ever share anything?

Because he's a little shellfish.

What kind of nut doesn't have a shell?

A doughnut.

What are two things you can never have for breakfast?

Lunch and dinner!

What's an astronaut's favorite chocolate?
Mars bars.

How do you cut the ocean in half?
With a sea-saw!

How do billboards talk to each other?
With sign language!

Why didn't the teddy bear eat dinner?
Because he was already stuffed!

What gets wetter the more it dries?

A towel.

Why should you never tell a joke to glass?

Because it might crack up!

How do you know when a bike is thinking?

Because its wheels will be turning!

What is a snake's favorite subject at school?

Hiss-tory.

What do sprinters eat before a race?

Nothing, they fast.

Why are bowling pins so sad?

Because they're always getting knocked down.

Where were pencils first invented?

Pencil-vania.

Why do penguins struggle to make new friends?

Because they can never break the ice.

Where do chefs learn to make ice cream?

At sundae school.

Why did the duck go broke?

Because his bill was too big.

What did Jack say to Jill when they finished rolling down the hill?

"Damn, I spilled the water!"

What's red and bad for your teeth?

A brick.

What do you call a vegetable when it retires?

A has-bean.

What's blue and smells like red paint?

Blue paint.

What type of music do balloons hate?

Pop.

Why can't your hand be 12 inches long?

Because then it would be a foot.

What time is it when a baseball goes through your window?

Time to get a new window.

What did one strand of DNA say to the other?

Do these genes make my butt look big?

Why should you never leave food around your computer?

It takes a lot of bytes.

Did you hear about the kidnapping in the park?

They woke him up.

What do cows like to read?
Cattle-logs.

What do you call a fly with no wings?
A walk.

What's the best thing to put into a pie?
Your teeth!

Where do horses live?
In NEIGH-borhoods.

What do cats eat for breakfast?

Mice krispies.

Why do computers never sleep?

They're always wired.

What did the buffalo say when his son left?

Bison!

What did the shark say when he ate a clown fish?

This tastes a little funny…

What is a boxer's favorite drink?

Punch!

What goes up but never comes down?

Your age.

Who gives sharks presents at Christmas?

Santa-jaws.

Why do bananas have to wear sunscreen when they go outside?

So they don't peel!

What do knights do if they're afraid of the dark?

They turn on the knight-light.

What did the duck say to the comedian?

You quack me up!

What do you call a hen that counts her eggs?

A mathemachicken!

What did one tomato say to the other?

Ketchup!

What do cats wear to bed?

Paw-jamas!

What did the hamburger name his daughter?

Patty.

How do you fix a broken tomato?

Tomato paste.

Where do bulls get their news?

From the bull-etin board.

What did the janitor say when he jumped out of the closet?

SUPPLIES!

Why did the man put his money in the freezer?

Because he wanted cold hard cash.

What do lawyers wear to work?

Law-suits.

What did one pencil say to the other?

You're looking sharp today!

How do you invite a dinosaur to lunch?

Tea, Rex?

What time should you go to the dentist?

Tooth-hurty!

What time is it when the clock strikes 13?

Time to get a new clock!

Why did the dog get in a fight?

Because it was a Boxer!

What did one flower say to the other?

Hi Bud!

What kind of clothes do kangaroos wear?

Jumpsuits.

What type of jam can't you eat?

A traffic jam!

Why did the scarecrow win an award?

Because he was outstanding in his field!

What's the difference between the bird flu and the swine flu?

One requires tweetment, and the other requires oinkment!

If athletes get athlete's foot, then what do elves get?

Mistle-toes.

What did the policeman say to his belly button?

You're under a vest!

How do rabbits travel?

By hareplane.

What do you call birds that stick together?

Vel-crows.

What do sea monsters eat?

Fish and ships.

What do you call a factory that sells good quality products?

Satisfactory.

Why did the barber win the race?

Because he knew a short cut.

Why does a chicken coup only have 2 doors?

Because if it had 4 doors it would be a chicken sedan.

What do you call a pile of cats?

A meow-tain!

Why don't they play blackjack in the jungle?

There are too many cheetahs!

What do you do with a sick boat?

Take it to the doc.

What's always running but never goes anywhere?

A refrigerator!

What did the horse say when it fell over?

Help, I can't giddy up.

Why do fish get bad grades?

Because they're below sea-level.

What kind of shoes do burglars wear?

Sneakers.

Why don't melons get married?

Because they cantaloupe.

Why shouldn't you tell jokes to eggs?

Because they might crack up!

Conclusion

Thanks again for choosing this book!

I hope you had fun making your friends and family laugh with all of the silly jokes!

www.ingramcontent.com/pod-product-compliance
Lightning Source LLC
LaVergne TN
LVHW021740060526
838200LV00052B/3389